M000266915

THE Green Wiccan YEAR

Celebrations·
Rituals·Herbal Magic·
Kitchen Witchery

By Silja

CICO BOOKS

LONDON NEW YORK

Published in 2018 by CICO Books
An imprint of Ryland Peters & Small
20–21 Jockey's Fields, London, WC1R 4BW
341 E 116th St, New York, NY 10029
www.rylandpeters.com

10 9 8 7 6 5 4 3 2 1

First Published in 2008 by CICO Books

Text © Silja Sample 2008
Design and illustration © CICO Books 2008

The author's moral rights have been asserted.
All rights reserved. No part of this publication
may be reproduced, stored in a retrieval
system, or transmitted in any form or by any
means, electronic, mechanical, photocopying,
or otherwise, without the prior permission of
the publisher.

A CIP catalog record for this book is available
from the Library of Congress and the British
Library.

ISBN: 978 1 78249 629 8

Printed in China

Editor: Samantha Gray
Designer: Roger Hammond
Illustrator: Michael Hill

this book belongs to

....

....

....

Magic can be done anywhere, anytime, with as many or as few ingredients as you have to hand, as is shown in my *Green Wiccan Book of Shadows*. However, timing does matter and as the energy for magic is drawn from Mother Nature, the seasons definitely influence what sort of rituals and magic a witch does, and what spells work best. For example, spring is a time for new beginnings in nature, and so a great time to start a new project in your own life too; summer is associated with the element of fire, the Sun God, and energizing your life and magic; fall is a time for harvesting and giving thanks for magic that worked, or finishing long term spells; and winter is associated with the element of water, and with introspection, studying new witchy subjects and meditation.

This book will help you improve your witchcraft skills and magical abilities with spells, rituals, meditations, and just little tips for all seasons of the year, as well as encourage you to work on your magical knowledge and spells. After all, witchcraft is a CRAFT, so the more you train and practice, the better you will get at your craft!

CONTENTS

Introduction 4

December and January
Yule and the Winter Solstice (December 21) 7

February
Imbolc (February 2) 27

March and April
Ostara and the Spring Equinox (March 22) 39

May
Beltaine (May 1) 59

June and July
Litha and the Summer Solstice (June 22) 71

August
Lughnasa and Lammas (August 1) 91

September
Mabon and the Autumn Equinox
(September 22) 103

October and November
Samhain and Halloween (October 31) 115

The Moon Rituals 134

Coven Notes 136
Spell Notes 140
Useful Websites and Acknowledgments 144

December and January

Yule and the Winter Solstice (December 21)

A SPELL TO GET OVER A BAD RELATIONSHIP

Make a garland by threading alternate pieces of popcorn (white, for the Goddess) and dried cranberries or red currants (red and round, for the Sun God) onto a cord; while you do this, think about the relationship and both its good and bad points, and how you will avoid the same issues reoccuring. Use the garland as decoration for your home during the Yule ritual and throughout the holiday season, then leave it outside for the birds to eat; as the birds gain energy from the food, negative feelings about the relationship will lessen and you will be ready to move on.

Midwinter is a time of celebration for many different religions, from the Buddhist "Festival of Lights," the Jewish Hannukkah, and the Christian Christmas to the Pagan Yule. Most Wiccans believe that Yule came first, as an ancient celebration of the days getting longer again as the Sun God returns, born of the Goddess who coupled with the God at Beltaine on May 1. It stays cold for some time yet, as the Goddess is tired after the birthing of the Sun God, and slumbers for a while before waking at Imbolc on 1st February, when spring starts.

YULE SYMBOLS

Many symbols associated with Christmas have a Wiccan origin. These include the Christmas tree, an ancient Pagan tradition revived by Queen Victoria in the nineteenth century. A Christmas tree combines the symbol of fertility and prosperity (the evergreen tree) with symbols of the Sun (red/gold baubles), the light becoming stronger again (candles), and faeries and elves (little figurines hung in the tree or, more recently, angel figures). The pentagram/star is placed at the top of the tree. Using holly to decorate your home represents the Holly King, ruler of the old, waning year. Mistletoe symbolizes the oak tree and the Oak King, ruler of the coming, waxing year. Evergreen branches, ivy, and pine cones are symbolic of rebirth and fertility, while red and gold ribbons introduce the colors of the God, and silver and white ones the colors of the Goddess.

The yule log, as the name suggests, is originally a Pagan custom too. It was once a wooden log rather than a chocolate one, and its burning in the fireplace or on a bonfire was a representation of the rebirth of the Sun God in the cleansing sacred fire of the Mother Goddess. Select a chunky log of oak or pine, making sure that it is dry so that it will burn a long time. Carve or chalk upon it a figure of the Sun and/or the Horned God. Set it alight in the fireplace at dusk on Yule, focusing on the goals for which you need energy in the next few months. When you wake the next morning to greet the reborn Sun God, there will hopefully still be some embers glowing.

December

1

2

3

4

5

6

7

8   Birthday of Dion Fortune, member of the Golden Dawn

9

10

11

CHANGE OF LUCK
To dispel bad luck, try this spell

Brew up a pot of tea using five teaspoonfuls of nutmeg and one cup of boiling water. Pour the tea into a bathtub and get in. While soaking in the bathtub, say this rhyme nine times:

"Change of luck come to me, as it will, so mote it be."

After each time, immerse yourself fully in the bath water. When you have finished soaking, take out the plug while still sitting in the bath and watch the water disappear down the drain. Imagine your bad luck and all negativity in your life disappearing down the plug hole with the water.

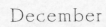
12

13

14

15

December

16

17

18

19

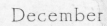

20

21

22

23

December

24

25

26

27

28

29

FRIDAY FOR LOVE

The day of Venus, the Goddess of Love, Friday is an excellent day for love magic.

30

31

Egyptian Lucky Day of Sehkmet

January

1

2

3

4

5

6

7

8

Birthday of MacGregor Mathers, one of the founders of Golden Dawn

January

9
Festival of Isis

10

11

12

13

14

15

CHOOSING A PARTNER
If you have feelings for two or more people, try this spell

On a New Moon, write the names of the people you are deciding between on separate pieces of white paper in blue (for wisdom) pen. In rows under each name, list the person's good and bad qualities. Leave another sheet of paper blank. Fold each piece of paper four times while saying:

"Lord and Lady help me see,
with whom I am meant to be.
Guide my hand and guide my heart
So my love may have a good start!"

Leave the folded pieces of paper somewhere safe until Full Moon, then shuffle them while repeating the chant four times. Open the top piece of paper. On it will be the name of the person you are meant to be with. If the paper is blank then you are meant to stay single for a while.

16

17

18

19

20

21

22

23

24

25

DISPEL
NEGATIVE
THOUGHTS
Black is used to
symbolize negativity, so
you might use a black
candle to burn away
negative thinking.

26

27

28

29

30

Birthday of Z Budapest, founder of Dianic Wicca

31

February

Imbolc (February 2)

A SPELL FOR REBIRTH

This spell recreates the extinguishing of the hearth fire, and will also get rid of negative energy people send you and even curses placed on you and members of your family:

Light a black candle in your cauldron that you filled with water, so the flame is about ½ an inch above the water. If you do not have a cauldron, use the kitchen basin. Say the following:
"Curses, negativity, leave us now, let us be!"

Watch the candle burn, and as the flame reaches the water level and extinguishes, the negativity will go away. Do not use this candle again, but instead bury it in a place you are unlikely to walk over.

Although it is unclear where the word "Imbolc" comes from, many Wiccans and scholars believe it comes from the Irish "folcaim," meaning washing, as the elders and spiritual leaders of Celtic times always took a ritual bath to purify themselves for the work ahead in the new season. They would wash away the grime of winter before spending the day observing the weather and wind patterns, which were thought to predict the weather over the following three months.

A FRESH START

Imbolc—Candlemas in Christianity—is when spring starts for Wiccans. It is a festival of hope and new beginnings, celebrating the coming of spring and the reawakening of Mother Nature. This is also a time for a proper spring clean—in Celtic times, this meant extinguishing the hearth fire, cleaning out the grate and relighting it (a big deal when no firelighters were available!). Nowadays, you can recreate this sense of renewal by clearing out stale energy and clutter from your home. Cleanse your home magically by smudging it—burning dried sage—then bless it by sprinkling rose water or burning frankincense.

THE MAIDEN GODDESS

During the celebration, the Maiden Goddess is worshipped and courted by the young, virile Hunter God, but it is not till the next fire Sabbat—Beltaine on May 1—that they will become a couple. In ancient Ireland, a bit of bread was left out for the Goddess Brigid, together with oats for her sacred white cow, in case she passed a home on her feast day. Then she would bless the home with prosperity and the women of the home with fertility. Brigid's Crosses are still made at this time of year, using wheat stalks, and you can find directions on how to make them in many books and on the internet.

Associated with new beginnings and the Maiden Goddess is the color white, so covens usually wear white robes, and warm milk with honey is often drunk during Imbolc rituals. After the ritual, those covens who are not vegetarian will enjoy fresh local lamb, harking back to ancient times when this was the first fresh meat of the season. Wiccans also buy or make their altar candle supply for the year before Imbolc, and bless these on the Sabbat.

February

1

2

3

4

5

6

7   Greek Day of Selene (Moon Goddess)

WHITE FOR ENERGY

Burn a white candle to
increase energy and give a
general boost to whatever
magic you might do.

February

8

Birth of Eliphas Lévi, French occult author and magician

9

10

11

12

Death of Gerald Gardner, a founding father of Wicca

13

Death of Cotton Mather, minister at the Salem Witch Trials

14

A SPELL

To help make your dreams come true, collect perfect bird's feathers when you see them on your travels (do not buy them!). Whenever you have nine feathers, tie them together with purple string and hang over a window or door frame in your home.

15

16

17

18

19

20

21

22

February

23

24

25

26

Egyptian Day of Nut (Goddess of healing and fertility)

27

28

29

ATTRACT MONEY

Placing three copper coins
under your front
door mat will help
to invite money
into the home.

March and April

Ostara and the Spring Equinox (March 22)

A SPELL FOR GOOD FORTUNE

To bring prosperity and good fortune into your life, get a little green potted tree or sturdy plant. Blow out five eggs, and color them in a color suitable to areas of your life which need help, such as pink for love, yellow for friendship, green for financial issues, blue for health, and red for sexual issues. Hang the eggs on the plant and place on your altar or table; after the festival, crush the eggshells and put them in the pot plant's soil for nourishment of the plant.

At this time of balance, when night and day are the same length, we give thanks for having come through the harsh winter, as well as through personal trials, and look forward to a warmer, more enjoyable summer. It's a time to take a quick break from mundane life to reflect upon the events of winter and to make plans, spiritual and otherwise, for the coming season. If you have been thinking about joining a coven, or attending a class on Wicca or fortune telling, now is the time to put your plans into action.

THE FESTIVAL OF RENEWAL

The Spring Equinox is closely tied to the preceding Sabbat, the fire festival of Imbolc—both are celebrations of renewal. Ostare, named after the German Goddess Eostre, focuses on prosperity and thanksgiving for new food and a new season of planting, whereas the theme for Imbolc is hope and the spiritual aspects of the season.

A symbol of new beginnings, and of being reborn, is the egg. Wiccans often decorate eggs with magical sygils and prosperity symbols such as hares—sacred to Eostre and a symbol of fertility— lambs, coins, and so on, then hang them outside their front doors to attract good luck for the coming seasons. If you prefer to eat your eggs, a popular way of decorating them is to stick magical herbs—camomile for healing, peppermint for good relations, or basil for money—and spring flowers onto white eggs. Place the eggs carefully in the heel of an old stocking and boil them in water colored with onion. The result is red-brown eggs decorated with the white outlines of herbs. Ostare is also a good time to perform any spells for prosperity and financial success, and to start long-term spells that will come to fruition by the Autumn Equinox.

Do not forget Mother Nature at this magical time of growth. Working magic and performing rituals indoors is wonderful, but take time out for a walk, ideally in the wilds of nature. However, if you cannot spare the time, a city park will do. Note the newly sprouting green grass, the budding trees and the first flowers of the season—gather some green foliage and seasonal flowers to decorate your home with!

March

1

Covenant of the Goddess, one of the largest Wiccan religious organizations, is formed

2

3

4

Celtic Feast of Rhiannon (Moon Goddess, Underworld Goddess)

5

6

7

8

9

Mother Goddess Day

10

11

12

IMPROVING YOUR RELATIONSHIP

To strengthen your relationship, try the following spell:

Cut a heart shape from red paper and sprinkle cinnamon onto it. Fold the heart shape three times, making sure that all the cinnamon stays wrapped inside. Bury it in the earth in a place that has special meaning for the two of you, such as where you met or had your first picnic.

Say:

"This spell bound and knotted tight as we walk upon this sight, keep us happy and safe with glee by Karmic power number three!"

13

14

Egyptian Festival of Au Set (Snake Goddess who wards off poverty)

15

16

17

18

19

20

21

22

23

BLUE FOR HEALING
For health magic, blue is the most prevalent color, as it symbolizes healing. Try burning a blue candle to boost your energy levels when you are feeling under the weather.

24

25

26

27

28

Death of popular Wiccan author Scott Cunningham

29

30

31

April

1

Feast Day of the Love Goddess, Venus

2

3

4

5

Feast Day of the Roman Goddess of Luck, Fortuna

6

7

8

9

10

Birthday of Montague Summers, witchcraft scholar

11

A SPELL TO SOLVE WORK PROBLEMS

Take a small clear glass bottle. Make sure it is totally clean, then fill it with a clove of garlic (for protection), a little sandalwood or sandalwood incense (to cleanse the atmosphere), and fill with rice (to symbolize the work/ business carrying on successfully).

Place the bottle in your desk drawer at the office and let it work its magic!

12

Cerealia , the eight-day annual festival in honor of the Fertility and Corn Goddess, Ceres, begins

13

14

15

16

17

18

19

20

21

22
Earth Day

MOVING HOUSE

Grate a little nutmeg and mix with cinnamon powder. Sprinkle a little on the front step of your house each morning and say:

"Quickly the house will be selling
Solid new buyers today will bring
This house was happy for us
for any new family it'll be a plus!"

Just before viewings, increase the power of the spell by baking something using cinnamon as an ingredient, or lighting some cinnamon incense.

23

Actress and spiritual author Shirley MacLaine is born

24

25

26

27

28

29

30 Walpurgis Night

May

Beltaine (May 1)

A POTION FOR LOVE

If you have your eye on someone but aren't sure they are interested, this drink will bring you closer together if you are meant to be; serve it at a party that the object of your affections will be at, or bring it to a birthday or leaving do at work!

To make the potion mix a quart (one liter) of pink champagne—or lemonade if you prefer non-alcoholic drinks—with a tablespoon of cinnamon and a teaspoon of red pepper. Add the core of a pomegranate to the mixture and stir clockwise. You can decorate with red and pink rose petals if available.

Beltaine (pronounced bell-t-A-n) is named after the fire god Bel. In mythology, it is the time when the virile young God and the Maiden Goddess get together and she conceives. This is probably why it has become a popular month to get married (a Wiccan wedding is called a handfasting), although in Wiccan mythology the two deities married at Lughnasad only when it became obvious that the Goddess was pregnant. Still, Beltaine has become a festival of love, relationships, and fertility—not just fertility for couples, but also for crops and animals. A symbolic public fertility ritual still practiced on many a village green is dancing around the maypole (a phallic symbol).

FESTIVAL OF FLOWERS

Even though Beltaine is the third and last of the spring celebrations, it is the biggest one. Finally it is really warm and Mother Nature is in full bloom—so much so that the Romans celebrated the festival of their Goddess Flora around this time. Wiccans have borrowed from that festival by decorating their altars and homes with whatever flowers and fresh green foilage they can find where they live. For those of us living in cities it is easier to buy flowers from a shop, but this is just not the same. Shop-bought flowers do not have the same natural energy as small, imperfect flowers plucked from your windowsill or garden.

THE MAY KING AND QUEEN

Beltaine is one of four fire festivals of the year, together with Lughnasa on August 1, Samhain on October 31, and Imbolc on February 1. It is traditional to light a fire during the ritual; if you do not have a fireplace or outdoor barbecue, try lighting a very small fire in your cauldron, or just light some candles. In covens, a spiritual play is staged during the Beltaine ritual. The coven chooses a May King—a willing male coven member—and a May Queen who is traditionally the youngest or newest female coven member. They dance together then jump over the fire—or over the South/fire elemental candle if the ritual is held indoors due to the weather or privacy—to bring luck to the coven in the coming year and ensure its prosperity. Afterwards, yeast bread—ideally baked in the coven's fireplace, or heart fire—is shared in the circle.

May

1

2

3

3rd–5th—Festival of the Roman Goddess, Flora

4

5

6

7

8

9

10

11

12

13

14

15

FIND A PARKING SPACE

There is a parking space faerie, and she likes chocolate! This is how to attract her:

Always have a piece of chocolate in your car.
When you need a parking space, chant:

"Parking faerie I am in a bind,
but a parking space I will find!"

Once you have parked,
drop the piece of
chocolate by the
sidewalk with thanks
to the parking faerie.

16

17

18

Feast of the Horned God

19

20

21

22

23

24

25

LUCKY CORAL

To banish negativity
and attract luck,
keep a small Goddess
statue made from
coral in your home.

26

27

28

29

30

31

June and July

Litha and the Summer Solstice (June 21)

A SPELL TO REMOVE NEGATIVITY AT WORK

To remove negativity and bad feelings at work, make a pentagram shape out of five blue pens or pencils (you can easily hide this in your drawer or at the back of your computer if necessary); as you lay each pencil down, say under your breath:

"Bad feelings are here, I am sorry to say. This spell will remove fear, and understanding will come, I pray!"

If there is one particular person that is the problem, arrange the pentagram so one of its points points directly to that person's desk/office.

Litha is the Anglo-Saxon name for roughly the same time of year as June. This is when the God and Goddess are strongest as a couple, and is a good time to do spells for strengthening a relationship, your career path, your spiritual resolve or whatever else you choose. Now may be the time to "come out of the closet" if you haven't shared your interest in Wicca with friends and family yet. It is also a time of completion—year-long spells might finish now, as might spiritual projects such as writing a magical diary, or learning a form of fortune telling. It is also a time for thanksgiving for spells that worked. The food for this Sabbat is honey cakes—deep-fried batter mixed with flower petals then dipped in honey while still warm. These make a great party food or a snack for a spiritual picnic with your friends.

A CELEBRATION OF THE SUN

This being the longest day, Wiccans celebrate by getting up just before dawn. After lighting a candle, the witch turns towards the horizon where the Sun will rise. A prayer is said to the Sun God to thank him for warmth and energy, and to ask for good weather. As the Sun rises in the sky, the candle is blown out; the same candle is then lit again at dusk, when the Sun disappears behind the visible horizon.

The Summer Solstice, the main celebration of the Sun God, and the next Sabbat, Lughnasa, the first harvest festival, are the big nature festivals. Try to spend at least some time outside with Mother Nature on such days. The Summer Solstice is the best time to see the "little folk"—faeries, elves, and goblins; traditionally, this was done by rubbing fern leaves into one's eyes at twilight or midnight. However, there are easier ways. Faeries can be found anywhere, but the most likely places are a faerie fort or hill, or a small stream overgrown and dark with foliage. Sit quietly, having placed some sweet offering—cookies or sugar cubes—by your side, and you might be lucky enough to see them. To attract faeries to your own home, place some facetted glass crystals in your windows so that the Sun's rays catch them and make rainbow patterns on your walls.

HERBS AND THEIR MAGICAL USES

ROSEMARY: purifies, great against nightmares, or put some in with your laundry to clean clothes from bad energy as well as dirt!

PEPPERMINT: Cleanses the stomach and the spirit.

GARLIC: protection against bad magic and negative people.

CATNIP: encourages a psychic bond with your pets (not just cats!).

MARJORAM: increases spirituality; drink as a herbal tea before meditation.

BASIL: The ultimate money herb—eat a dish with basil before going to see your bank manager!

LAVENDER: relaxes; put a few sprigs in your coat pocket before a stressful business meeting.

LEMON BALM: healing, and a mild natural antidepressant.

CAMOMILE: Helps you sleep and forget your troubles.

June

1

England's Witchcraft Act of 1563 is passed, banning the practice of witchcraft

2

3

4

5

Earth Mother Day

6

7

8

June

9

10

11

ROSE FOR BLESSING

To bless a new home or magical
tool, sprinkle it with rose water.
You can make your own by
putting a few fragrant rose
petals, or rose essential oil, into
a bottle of mineral water.

12

13

Birthday of Gerald Gardner, widely regarded as the founder of Wicca

---

14

15

Margaret Jones is the first person to be executed as a witch in Massachusetts

---

16

17

18

19

20

21

22

England's last Witchcraft Law is repealed in 1951

23

Day of the Faerie Goddess

24

25

26

27

Birthday of influential Wiccan author Scott Cunningham

28

29

30

AMBER FOR HARMONY

To promote a positive working
or family environment after a
disagreement, wear a piece
of amber.

July

1

2

3

4

5

6

7

8

9

10

SUNDAYS AND MONDAYS

If you are doing a love spell to attract a man, Sunday—day of the Sun God and all male aspects of deity—is auspicious.

Alternatively, if you want to attract a woman, do your spell on Monday, the day of the Moon Goddess and femininity.

11

12

13

14

15

16

17

18

19

Rebecca Nurse is accused of being a witch and hanged in Salem, Massachusetts in 1692

20

21

22

23

ATTRACT SUCCESS

Tiger's eye is the stone to wear for
business success. Keep it with you
to help you on new ventures and
give you the confidence to
maximize your potential.

24

25

26

27

28

29

30

31

August

Lughnasa and Lammas (August 1)

A SPELL FOR FRIENDSHIP

Sometimes a friend may ask you to perform magic to help them, but they cannot be present or do not wish to perform magic themselves; in such cases, this spell is appropriate: Get a white piece of paper and write the friend's name on one side, and on the other side of the paper, write what they need help with. Roll the paper up in a corn husk. Then use more corn husks to make a rough human shape around the paper, so the paper is in the middle (the "belly") of the corn dolly. Carefully choose the color of the string you use to make the corn dolly to be appropriate to the spell (blue for healing, green for general prosperity and fertility, yellow or gold for finances, etc). Place the corn dolly on your altar or in a sunny spot on the windowsill until the issue the friends asked help with is resolved.

Lughnasa (pronounced "lu-na-sa") is the first of the harvest festivals and, if at all possible, should be celebrated outdoors. If this is not possible, decorate the altar with wheat, barley, and/or oats, and the first fruit of the season. Lughnasa is a time of celebration and thanksgiving for the great bounty of food Mother Nature gives us with the help of Father Sun who provides the light and warmth. Even if you do not normally pray before meals, a short prayer of thanks is appropriate on this day—you can model this on the Christian version: "For what we are about to receive, may the Lord and Lady make us truly thankful!" Add some personal thanks for the good things that have happened to you lately and for the particular food you are about to eat.

A TIME FOR CELEBRATION

Food plays a major part in the Lughnasa Sabbat. Covens often have a pot-luck dinner after their ritual, to which everyone brings a delicious dish made with local, seasonal ingredients. If you are not a member of a coven, you can still do this and invite your friends around! After the dinner, a more elaborate version of the Earth Offering ritual is performed, with the seeds of fruit that has been eaten sown back in the earth in thanks and to symbolize the circle of life and rebirth.

Lughnacy games are another aspect of the celebrations at this Sabbat. Adults resurrect their favorite simple childhood games such as hopscotch and playing catch, and compete against each other in friendly competitions. The winner is rewarded with a crown made from corn stalks. Corn is also eaten as corn on the cob, baked in the embers of the bonfire from the ritual and slathered with butter. It is used, too, for making corn dollies for children to play with and to put on the altar to represent coven members and family who cannot be present at the celebrations.

In mythology, Lughnasa is sacred to the Celtic God Lugh, who instituted the first celebrations in honor of Tailtiu, the Queen of the Fir Bolg. Tailtiu worked until she died from exhaustion to make the land ready for the planting of wheat and corn for the humans under her care. As she lay dying, she promised the people that, as long as they honored her memory by celebrating, they would always have food in body and mind—some say this is the reason the Irish are so well known for their literary and artistic achievements.

August

1

2

3

Day of the Dryads (maiden spirits of wood and water)

4

5

6

7

8

9

Druid Feast of the Fire Spirits

10

11

CALMING CHANT

After a stressful day or when having difficulty with someone, brew a cup of tea;
as you stir in milk or sugar clockwise, say the following chant:

"I seek prosperity and calm
and so I prepare this balm
I only seek what is right,

as I drink, my wishes take flight.
As this tea I ingest,
Lord and Lady, help me rest."

12

13

14

15

August

16

17

18

19

20

21

22

23

August

24

25

26

27

28

29

BANISHING ENEMIES

If someone wishes you ill but won't leave you alone, write his or her name with a blue pen on a white piece of paper. Place the paper in a small bowl of water and put in the very back of your freezer. Leave the bowl there for at least one lunar month to literally freeze the person out of your life.

30

31 Birthday of author Raymond Buckland, credited with introducing Wicca to the United States

September

Mabon and the Autumn Equinox (September 22)

A SPELL FOR STRENGTH

Totem animals can help increase your confidence in all situations as you take their energy and particular strengths inside you. To gain a totem animal, pick an animal that embodies what you are looking to do (panther for quiet strength, eagle for not caring too much, sparrow for adaptability, etc) and get a photo or drawing of the animal. Stick this on a mirror just above eye-level (bathroom mirrors work great for this). Light a plain beeswax candle (a white candle will do if you cannot find beeswax) and stand in front of the mirror with it. Look into the candle flame and envisage situations and problems where you may need the strength the animal symbolizes. When you feel yourself becoming uncomfortable, nervous or afraid, look up at the totem animal and take strength from it. If you feel the need for extra energy even after this spell, place the picture of the totem animal in your wallet or purse so it is always with you.

Like the Spring Equinox, balance is celebrated at this Sabbat. The Sun God is waning and the Goddess is sad about the impending loss of her consort, but she is also joyous because she is heavily pregnant and will give birth to the next Sun God at Yule. The altar is decorated with autumn leaves to symbolize the waning Sun God. (Dip the leaves in paraffin if you'd like to use them for a long time.) Apples, grapes, carrots, potatoes, and home-made cider represent the Mother Goddess still being strong. Pomegranates, sacred to the Goddess Persephone, are also used as decorations—a theme of Mabon is death and the underworld, which is not to be feared due to the prospect of rebirth. Deep meditations and rituals to overcome great difficulties, and say goodbye to loved ones who departed from this world in the past year, are often performed at this Sabbat.

PROTECTION AND HUNTING

Spells for protection, security, wealth, and prosperity are performed at Mabon. If you are afraid of vandals, now is the time to make a witch bottle to bury at the threshold of your home. For greater security over money or your job, guard against potential issues with a magical spell.

This is also a time for hunting, because the ancient witches believed that, by eating an animal's flesh, you would also take into yourself its energy and strength—for example, becoming as majestic as a stag. If you eat meat, celebrate this time with some local wild meats, such as pheasant or venison, or go fishing, or even hunting. However, you do not need to consume meat to celebrate the hunt. Instead, you could attend a demonstration of birds of prey, meditate upon a photograph or drawing of a wild animal, or "hunt" for feathers in the park with which to decorate your altar.

Prepare for the coming winter spiritually and in craft ways by going for long walks in nature, reflecting upon the summer that has gone and what you'd like to do this winter. During your walk, gather nuts, berries to conserve, and apples to dry in readiness for winter when there is no fresh produce.

September

1

2

3

4

September

5

6

7

8

September

9

10

11

12

13
Egyptian Lighting of the Fire Ceremony (for spirits of the dead)

14
Birthday of the medieval magician and occult author Cornelius Agrippa

15

BOOST TO HEALTH

To keep healthy, place a photograph of yourself in front of a blue candle. Light the blue candle and some incense. Close your eyes and take three deep breathes, then open them again. Looking at your photograph, make three slow clockwise circles around it with the incense while saying this chant:

"Keep me healthy and illness free as I will it, so mote it be!"

Then pass the incense over yourself, chanting again:

"Keep me healthy and illness free as I will it, so mote it be!"

September

16

17

18

19

20

21

22

23

24

25

26

LOVE SPELL

For this love spell, you will need a pink candle, a piece of white paper, and a red pen. Light the candle. Think about the qualities you are looking for in a partner, and write them down. Be realistic—while the spell may increase your chances of meeting a billionaire, it's still unlikely! Do NOT write down a specific person's name, because this spell will draw a good, loving partner to you, and is not designed to bind a particular person to you—that would be black magic. When you are ready, say the following:

"If there be a perfect match,
this work tonight will surely catch.
The perfect one who is meant to be,
shall find his way home to me.

In perfect love and perfect trust,
I send this out, but not from lust,
This spell will guide us to unite,
free will remains with us tonight."

27

28

29

30

October and November

Samhain and Halloween (October 31)

APPLE SPELL

Hold an apple in your left hand next to your heart, and a knife in your right hand. Think about a question that can be answered by a yes or no, me or others. Cut the apple horizontally—not along the core, but from side to side. You will see five pips in the shape of a pentagram—a five-pointed star. If one of the pips points directly away from you, the answer to your question is no/others; if one points directly toward your heart, the answer is yes/you.

In mythology, this is the time when Mother Earth goes into confinement, wrapping herself in a white coat of snow, to give birth to the Sun God yet again at Yule, the Winter Solstice. The main theme of Samhain is the connection between this world and other worlds. It is a great time for getting in touch with ghosts, as well as to go on vision quests and guided meditations. Fortune telling at New Year to gain a glimpse of the coming year is also popular.

The altar is decorated with the symbols of the last of the harvest—nuts, apples, and pumpkins —and beautifully colored leaves.

WICCAN MEDITATIONS

Meditation has many benefits, and Wiccans use it for purposes, ranging from raising energy levels to calming the mind to help focus on tasks and rituals. Try out these meditations:

Simple Meditation

Sitting comfortably, breathe in through your nose, imagining good energy entering your body. Now exhale through the mouth to dispel negative energy.

Intermediate Meditation

The "happy place" meditation will help to calm you when you feel stressed, angry, or sad. Start by sitting comfortably or lying down, and closing your eyes. Imagine a place in nature that you love—not an actual place you know but a fantasy of your ideal place. This could be under a big tree on top of a hill, in the middle of a cornfield, or on a sandy beach. Imagine every detail of this place—feel the moss under your feet, hear the birds singing, or smell the salty air from the sea. Repeat the visualization many times until it is exactly how you want it. Whenever you have a free moment, visit this happy place in your mind. Initially, it will take a little effort and concentration, but soon your mind will be able to escape to your happy place easily. You can then go there for a moment's relaxation before that big business meeting—or when your three year old is being a pain!

Advanced Meditation

Guided meditations are a great way to advance your practice. With someone else talking it is easier to follow the words and relax into a deep meditative state. There are many CDs and tapes available with all kinds of guided meditations. Even better, get together with friends each week, taking it in turns to print out a meditation from a book or the internet—or write an original one—and talk the others through it.

Vision quests are another form of advanced meditation in which you travel deep into your subconcious to find out what to do about an issue, or form a connection with a deity or spirit to help you with a goal in your life. This can be unsettling at first, and I would recommend that you become familiar with more basic forms of meditation, and hone your intuition and knowledge of Wiccan spirituality, before engaging in a vision quest.

1

Birthday of Isaac Bonewits, influential Neopagan author

2

3

PUMPKIN WITCHERY

Carving pumpkins originates from the tradition of carving turnips in the old days. Ghoulish faces were carved to scare away malevolent spirits and ghosts, but you can also make your pumpkins or turnips smile to invite in good spirits and make visitors to your home happy.

4

October

5

6

7

8

October

9

10

11

12

13

14

Patricia Crowther, one of the early mothers of Wicca is born

15

16

October

17

18

19

20

21

22

23

A SPELL TO DRAW IN MONEY
Here is an easy money spell to help towards winter expenses

Take three basil leaves and three copper coins. Place each coin on a leaf, saying:

"Gold and green
little money I have seen
Now I draw money to me
for the best this may be!"

Then eat the three leaves, and put the coins in your wallet. Make sure that at least one of the coins always stays in your wallet, and it will draw more money toward it!

24

25

26

27

28

29

30

31

November

1

Day of the Banshees

2

3

Petronella De Meath is executed in the first recorded Witch Burning in Ireland, 1324

REVITALIZING HERB TEA

Prepare this tea as a pick-me-up and to
balance your emotions. You can make a
whole bag of the mixture and then brew
a cup whenever you feel
the need:

- 2 parts peppermint
- 1 part camomile
- 1 part fennel

4

5

6

7

8

9

10

11

Celtic Lunatishees (Day of the Faerie Sidhe)

12

13

14

15

16

Night of Hecate (Goddess of the Moon, Magic, and Witches)

17

18

19

20

21

22

23

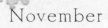

November

24

25

26

27

28

_____

29

Egyptian Feast of Hathor (as Sehkmet, the Alternated Bast)

_____

30

Birthday of Oberon Zell-Ravenheart, founder of the Church of All Worlds

_____

KNOT SPELL

A simple knot spell can be used to help your goals and plans come to fruition.
Take a piece of cord and tie nine knots into it while saying:

"By the knot of one, this spell is begun!
By the knot of two, my spell comes true
By the knot of three, so mote it be.
By the knot of four, power I store
By the knot of five, my magic is alive
By the knot of six, this spell I fix

By the knot of seven, this spell I leaven.
By the knot of eight, if it is fate
By the knot of nine, what I wish is mine!"

Leave the knotted cord somewhere safe until
you reach your goal.

The Moon Rituals

Full Moon Rituals

A SPELL FOR STRENGTH

Called Esbats, Full Moon rituals are the traditional meeting day for covens. The Moon's energy is at its strongest is when it is full, favoring spells and magical rituals. In days gone by, there was also a more practical consideration —covens used to meet in forest clearings or on top of hills at night, and when there was no electrical light, the Full Moon helped to guide the way. You do not have to be part of a coven to celebrate the Full Moon—it serves as a useful reminder for any Wiccan to practice their spirituality and take a monthly time-out from the mundane world.

THE RITUAL PROCESS

A Full Moon ritual can be as simple or as complex as you wish. For example, it's nice to have a special ritual robe to wear but it's not essential. Always start by casting a circle—making a ritual space. One way to perform magic in this ritual is to light candles symbolizing the four elements. Then begin to gather energy. Visualize energy rising from the ground (Mother Earth) and descending from the sky (Father Sun). Perform or renew any spells you wish. The Full Moon is also a time to give thanks for magic that worked, so don't forget to say a prayer of thanksgiving to the deities and spirits, and any spiritual teachers, real or on the astral plane, who helped you on your path during the last month.

Once the magic is done, it is traditional to ground oneself by having something to eat and drink. This is called the "cakes and ale" part of the Esbat ritual, since oat cakes and home-brewed ale used to be shared around the coven circle. These days, it might be cookies and elderflower lemonade! In any case, ensure you leave a little drink in the cup for the earth offering. When you are done, do not forget to close your magical circle and give thanks to the Earth Mother with an earth offering—pour the rest of the drink over a plant in your garden or on your window sill. This liquid possesses potent magic, so pour it over plants, such as herbs, you are growing for spells, or over a holly bush.

New Moon Rituals

The New Moon is the time of the Crone or wise woman. This is traditionally when the Elders gather to discuss spiritual matters. They also now take time to work with their hands rather than their minds—in other words, this is when the "craft" of witchcraft takes precedence over the "witch," or magic, part. Covens who have the time to meet twice a month will spend the New Moon making candles, cleansing their ritual tools and sewing robes for festivals. Busy training covens often meet twice a month—the whole coven gathering on the Full Moon and just the more experienced members of the coven (those already initiated) on the New Moon. This gives experienced witches a chance to practice more complicated spells and discuss the progress of newer, probationary coven members. These rituals are held among a trusted group of people who have usually known each other for years, and so are often held skyclad (naked). This is not for any sexual reason, but to symbolize that we are clothed in the cloak of the Sky Goddess, and that we are all equal, whether we can afford expensive ritual robes or not.

The Babylonians thought the New Moon was the time the Goddess was menstruating, and thus prepared for a new cycle. Magically, the New Moon is the time for new beginnings. It is the time to start spells that will come to fruition at the next Full Moon. If you want to begin a new project or try a new craft, then start now. Alternatively, experiment with a new type of meditation or a tea made from magical herbs. Prepare a magical garden at the New Moon, planting it as the Moon starts to wax. As the Moon grows in the sky, so your plants will grow. If you like working magic outdoors, find a new, private location to practice the next Esbat ritual. As this is a dark time of the month, it is also an occasion to perform banishing rituals. Such rituals are not black magic, but help everyone by removing negative energy such as aggression and bad thoughts among people. So if you feel someone "has it in for you" where you work, or has even cursed you—curses are very rare, but they do happen—or if you simply want to stop your own negative thought patterns, them perform a suitable spell or write an uplifting chant.

Coven notes

Use these pages to make notes at your coven meetings or to write down questions or thoughts you would like to bring up at your next gathering.

Coven notes

Spell notes

Use these pages to make a note of any new spells or rituals you have learnt or would like to try out.

Use

_____

_____

Ingredients

_____

_____

Special instructions

_____

_____

Use

_____

_____

Ingredients

_____

_____

Special instructions

_____

_____

Use

_____

_____

Ingredients

_____

_____

Special instructions

_____

_____

Use
_____

Ingredients
_____
_____

Special instructions
_____
_____

Use
_____

Ingredients
_____
_____

Special instructions
_____
_____

Use
_____

Ingredients
_____
_____

Special instructions
_____
_____

Spell notes

Use

_____

_____

Ingredients

_____

_____

_____

Special instructions

_____

_____

_____

Use

_____

_____

Ingredients

_____

_____

_____

Special instructions

_____

_____

_____

Use

_____

_____

Ingredients

_____

_____

_____

Special instructions

_____

_____

Use

Ingredients

Special instructions

Use

Ingredients

Special instructions

Use

Ingredients

Special instructions

Useful Websites

Beginner Wicca
Contains useful information for those just
starting out in the Wiccan world
www.beginnerwicca.com

The Celtic Connection
One of the largest sites on the internet
dedicated to Wicca
www.wicca.com

The Good Wiccan
A great resource aimed at beginner
solo practitioners
www.goodwiccan.com

The Pagan Federation
Informative UK site
www.paganfed.org

The Witches Voice
Provides news and educational information
for witches and Wiccans
www.witchvox.com

Acknowledgments

I would like to thank the Power for my great husband and wonderful children,
the true blessings in my life.